Zodiac Dogs

Zodiac Dogs

The astrology of dogs and their owners

Jane Lang

Zambezi Publishing Ltd

First published in 2023 in the UK by Zambezi Publishing Ltd
Plymouth, Devon PL2 2EQ
Tel: +44 (0)1752 367 300
email: zambezipub@gmail.com   www.zampub.com

British Library Cataloguing in Publication Data:
A catalogue record for this book is available from the British Library

ISBN(13) 978-1-903065-97-6
Illustrations copyright © 2023:
Jane Lang, Dreamstime.com,
Cover image Jan Budkowski, Jane Lang
Typesetting by Zambezi Publishing Ltd, Plymouth

Disclaimer:- This book is intended to provide general information
regarding the subject matter, and to entertain. The contents are not
exhaustive and no warranty is given as to accuracy of content. The book
is sold on the understanding that neither the publisher nor the author
are thereby engaged in rendering professional services, in respect of the
subject matter or any other field. If expert guidance is required, the
services of a qualified professional should be sought.
Readers are urged to access a range of other material on the book's
subject matter, and to tailor the information to their individual needs.
Neither the author nor the publisher shall have any responsibility to any
person or entity regarding any loss or damage caused or alleged to be
caused, directly or indirectly, by the use or misuse of information
contained in this book. If you do not wish to be bound by the above,
you may return this book in original condition to the publisher, with its
receipt, for a refund of the purchase price.

About the Author

Coming from a career in Dance and Performance Art, Jane was taught to draw at age four by her East European mother. She has an Honours Degree in Fine Art from Central St Martins and her art work lives all over the world from the USA to the Middle East.

During the lockdown she lost her beloved husband Colin. They shared a mutual fascination in the natural world, from the tiniest creature to the solar system itself – the whole magical universe of which humans are just a part.

Fascinated by medieval astrological writings, Jane also trained with the British Astrological and Psychic Society (BAPS) as an astrologer, drawing 3D versions of astrological charts for clients. Colin and Jane were working on astrological and art projects when he died. This book came out of a game they played together which involved their love of astrology and animals, and large dollops of humour!

Dedication

This book is for Colin.

Zodiac Dogs

Contents

Introduction

This book was born out of laughter and love. My darling, late husband Colin and I shared a love of many things, including dogs and astrology. Merging the two was becoming a twelve-page download for an unusual business we had in mind, and the idea came out of a game we used to play. The game centred on what would happen if, for example, an Aries dog was teamed up with a Virgo owner. As it happens, Colin was a Virgo - as am I - and we knew we would have difficulty with some of the livelier doggie star sign types of pooch.

We would laugh out loud at different dog and owner permutations, and while we were out walking, we would try to guess the zodiac signs of the dogs we passed and of their owners. There were many chuckles, such as: "Ooooh look, that's a Leo dog with a Taurus owner!" Sometimes we would just look at each other and mouth "Capricorn" as the hound passed us by. It was the greatest fun!

Colin had introduced me to astrology and had guided me through learning to calculate the charts by hand, but during the lockdown, I would show him the drawings of dogs I had done, which meant the chuckles continued even when we were keeping away from other people.

Introduction

Then spring came along with sunny weather, and we were planning on getting a dog for ourselves once the Covid situation had eased, but suddenly, and with no warning, my darling boy died of a heart attack, after which the notes and drawings went into a drawer.

Time passes whether you want it to or not, so a couple of years later when I was talking to the wonderful Sasha Fenton, I remembered our ideas and the laughter that went with them. With her encouragement, I began to write and draw around the basic idea of the astrology of dogs and their owners. It has given me the greatest pleasure to revisit the joy I shared with Colin; and at times, even when very sad, I found myself eying a dog in the street and I could sense him around me and hear his infectious laughter in the background as I thought to myself, "Virgo".

K9 Tips
First-time pet owner?
Get your puppy from a sound,
recognised breeder.
Don't just go for any unverified
newspaper advert.

Sun Sign Aries

Dates: March 21 to April 19
Planet: Mars
Symbol: The Ram
Gender: Masculine
Element: Fire
Quality: Cardinal
Colour: Red
Gem: Jasper

The Aries Dog

March 21 to April 19

This dog bounds up and down and all over. There is enthusiasm and energy here that will need to be trained from day one, if not earlier! You will find yourself laughing at your courageous and intrepid Aries dog as it leads you up hill and down dale, and often into puddles, barking contests and embarrassing situations. They love to be the first at everything, so be warned. Whether jumping for a treat or chasing a squirrel, they will strive to get there ahead of you and everyone else, as if their life depended on it.

As well as being adorable, friendly and lovable, your Aries pet has a shadow side that is inconsiderate, clumsy and egocentric. You think it didn't hear you? It did, but it decided to ignore you!

Just remember to train, train and train!

The Aries Dog

The Aries Owner

March 21 to April 19
Say hello to Aries, the first sign of the zodiac, capable of wild, impulsive behaviour and possessed of a seemingly inexhaustible supply of energy. Lovely when they are inspirational and go-getting, but not so hot when they tip over into arrogance and reckless behaviour.

So, what sort of dog would appeal to our self-sufficient Aries owner? An adventurous companion, particularly in younger years, a dog that can amuse itself and isn't too needy might be just the ticket. In later years, should "Burn Out" occur, a steadfast and calm companion could help nurture a frazzled Aries soul and would build an unbreakable bond.

Features

Love: Aries folk are direct and with their famous independence, can make for stimulating and lively romantic mates. They are passionate and love living life in the moment. An aside… if you love them, you will have to love their dog too.

Money: For Aries, freedom of expression, a lack of constraint and a horror of boredom will figure highly in any career option – so money may come and go. With the right formula, it will stay. They need an adaptable canine companion, equally at home in a castle or a caravan.

Health: All that energy and ferocity of spirit can eventually take a toll with periods of exhaustion if our Aries are not careful to factor in time to replenish and nurture themselves. A dog cuddle when energy levels are low can be a great tonic and morale booster!

K9 Tips
Make sure your new pet is
vaccinated and healthy.
Let your local Vet. check it out.

Sun Sign Taurus

Dates: April 20 to May 20
Planet: Venus
Symbol: The Bull
Gender: Feminine
Element: Earth
Quality: Fixed
Colours: Pink and green
Gem: Emerald

The Taurus Dog

April 20 to May 20

This is a pleasure-loving dog, and a good roll in some poo followed by a good cuddle and an equally good feed is exactly what this dog loves. It is stable and reliable and will love you, come what may. A good dog if you're feeling stressed; its mere presence will calm you down. Also, this dog loves physical contact, tummy rubs and all. They are reliable; what you see is what you get. In return for its soothing influence, remember to give this creature the stability it craves – don't move its bed around, and if you have to move home, this dog will probably need counselling!

They are generally not sprinters, preferring to plod and smell the roses and everything else. If you rush them too much, they will respond by going more slowly, and if you still persist, you can face them grinding to an absolute halt.

Vary their routine from time to time to stop them becoming stuck in their ways, and as they age, keep up stimulating activities. Treats can work wonders – just don't use this tactic too often, because their waistlines can make them even less inclined to move!

Stabilise, stabilise, stabilise!

The Taurus Dog

The Taurus Owner

April 20 to May 20

Now we meet the zodiac sign of Taurus. Earthy, grounded and persistent, these are people you can rely on, both to be there for you and to get things done. Taureans like to feel secure and make their way through life in a steady, sometimes agonisingly slow way. They have a deeply sensuous side, so dog cuddling will appeal from the word go! A loving, loyal dog which enjoys sleeping by the fire, curling up on its owner's lap, and taking one look at the rain outside and going back to sleep will appeal. However, when Taureans are low, they can slide into depression, and having to get up and walk a dog and being forced to play the occasional tug of war can help lift Taurean spirits out of the doldrums.

Features

Love: This is an affectionate sign and familiarity just breeds love and more love. Taureans revel in the day-to-day contentment that a long-term relationship brings, both with humans and dogs. They will enjoy a steadfast, dependable and loving dog. Snappy divas need not apply.

Money: Although Taureans may not go after glory, they will go after security, and they work steadily to ensure they take care of all their basic needs. This is a productive and hard-working sign. A dog that can learn simple commands and obey instructions will go down a treat.

Health: Taureans are vulnerable to colds and sore throats, and they need to keep their immune system up to scratch, as they can be prone to arthritis. Walking the dog on a regular basis both combats the danger of falling into low moods and introduces the discipline of regular exercise.

K9 Tips
Get your pet chipped:
Don't let pet thieves win.

Sun Sign Gemini

Dates: May 21 to June 21
Planet: Mercury
Symbol: The Twins
Gender: Masculine
Element: Air
Quality: Mutable
Colours: Yellow
Gem: Citrine

The Gemini Dog

May 21 to June 21

These are mega bright dogs. Hyperactivity is their middle name, and they will keep you on your toes. They wake up quickly! Inquisitive to their core, you will need to engage that quick brain as soon as you can, or you will find their boredom and frustration can lead to chewed furniture, destroyed plastic bins and death to all papers left lying around. Be inventive with them and enjoy and participate in their cleverness, or their quickness will outwit you. They can get impatient, so never overlook a good walk every day.

Tire them out and make them puzzle things out, and you will have a delightful companion. They can be a bit fickle if they start to consider you boring, so they can be lured off to new connections that seem more enticing. Don't be hurt by this, because it's their nature. If they see you as stimulating and you can hold their attention, you'll be theirs for keeps. However, make sure they get their down time because they can get overactive and frazzled. It will be up to you as pack leader to ensure there is a balance in this clever and engaging dog's life.

Engage, engage, engage!

The Gemini Dog

The Gemini Owner

May 21 to June 21
Next on our zodiac list is the fun-loving Gemini. This is a clever and quick-witted sign. Fascinated by the new and enlivened by the unexpected, vastly amusing to be around and yet strangely tiring at times to the rest of us. Constant curiosity makes Geminis lively companions, and a challenging dog could pique this sign's interest. The latest breed, the most fashionable dog around, the most eccentric behaviour is all grist to the Gemini mill.

A dog that just wants a quiet life lying in front of the fire won't do here. The downside of the charming Gemini is a certain fickleness and a tendency to getting bored quickly, so learning new training techniques as well as new tricks for the hound in question should keep Geminis interested. Training is crucial, as there may not be room for two divas in one house!

Features

Love: Geminis have been accused of being fickle. However, as long as their partner can keep their interest, stimulate them and have enough self-belief to allow this sign the long lead they need, all will be well. These necessary traits apply to their dog as well!

Money: Clever, versatile and easily bored Geminis can master skills in a trice and delight in pursuing new ideas. These are the inventive entrepreneurs par excellence! If they can learn that they are not massively good with managing money themselves, hopefully they can draw in financial guidance.

Health: Sudden changes of mood and a tendency to do too many things at once can scatter our Gemini's energy and make them anxious. Having an animal to care for and love is a good focus for those days when things get on top of this mercurial sign.

K9 Tips
Always use a good Vet., regularly.

Sun Sign Cancer

Dates:	June 22 to July 22
Planet:	The Moon
Symbol:	The Crab
Gender:	Feminine
Element:	Water
Quality:	Cardinal
Colour:	Silver
Gem:	Moonstone

The Cancer Dog

June 22 to July 22

This dog is emotionally out there! It wears its heart on its breast, so to speak, and it will tune in to you as no one has done before. These dogs know you are down before you do, and they will start wagging their tails before you realise how happy you are. You are their sun and moon and all things in between. They will never leave you or give up on you. This dog has an astounding memory, which can be useful when training the dog, and it can be very determined, so never underestimate it.

Cancer dogs have a powerful longing for your love and to be the centre of your life, whether you want them there or not. So, establish sensible boundaries and do it pretty sharply, or they can take being stopped from doing something as a rejection and go into a depressive slump. If you don't set reasonable and kind limits, they will commandeer your bed, you will be the only human or animal allowed in, and they will want to protect you to the death! This is a determined, not to say obsessive, dog and trust me - you don't want to be the sole object of its obsession! With good give and take, though, you will have the most loyal pet ever.

Control, control, control!

The Cancer Dog

The Cancer Owner

June 22 to July 22

The sign of the Crab is protective outside and soft inside. One of the most caring and loving Signs of the zodiac, Cancer never gives up on anyone, and very importantly, never gives up on any dog.

Needing to create a stable, tranquil home and enjoy domestic harmony, any dog would be welcome and nurtured here. This is where a rescue dog would find its salvation, and the love that is returned would nurture our Cancerian in return.

The sensitive, vulnerable part of Cancer that can plummet into anxiety can benefit from the adoration of a dog. Possessiveness can work both ways between a dog and its owner, and the right match here can help to save both human and dog.

Features

Love: Cancer lives to cherish and love. Break-ups can be devastating, though having that shell to hide in and heal in helps. Maternal (no matter what sex) and nurturing, this is a super caring sign. However, a small warning - the Cancerian must watch that their dog's waistline doesn't grow too big!

Money: Being emotionally acute can stand Cancerians in good stead in many fields, and their ability to give their all can lead to professional success. Often a leader, they bring a sense of family along with them, ensuring financial stability.

Health: Getting overwhelmed and suffering from mood swings are Cancerian challenges and having a constant, loving dog companion can help to recharge those caring batteries. A dog can provide the place of calmness, love and cuddles that a frazzled Cancerian requires.

K9 Tips
Use top quality flea treatment and spray.
Many cheap versions don't work that well.

Sun Sign Leo

Dates: July 23 to August 22
Planet: The Sun
Symbol: The Lion
Gender: Masculine
Element: Fire
Quality: Fixed
Colour: Gold
Gem: Topaz

The Leo Dog

July 23 to August 22

Well, you have canine royalty here. With heads held high, these dogs expect adoration, good food and the best seats in the house! They won't just want to sit on the new sofa, they will perch on the highest point and survey their kingdom with complete confidence while attracting admiring glances as if it is their due, because they are born expecting the very best. They expect to light up a room, and light up a room they will. Grooming is accepted as an inevitable inconvenience, and they will expect you to measure up.

Although canine royalty, this is a loyal and loving dog. They love to love you and will be there for you through thick and thin. However, your Leo dog does expect to have the best foodstuffs to eat, so no cheap, cut-price tins or packets of down-market stuff will do.

Despite their generous nature, they are capable of real sulks and drama queen or king behaviour, so make sure you give them absolute love, praise (even when it's not warranted!) and the cuddles they know are their absolute due. Love them and they will love you back.

Cuddle, cuddle, cuddle!

The Leo Dog

The Leo Owner

July 23 to August 22

You will always know when there's a Leo in the room. Exuding confidence, they will instinctively take the space they feel is theirs by right, and they will draw everyone into their orbit. Leos are courageous, generous and creative when at their best, though susceptible to flattery, prone to exaggeration and arrogant at their worst. They need praise for their achievements, and their dog would need to be worthy of them, too. Doggie looks might count, but also the doggie story with which our Leo can regale an audience will also matter. The prize pedigree, the brave canine, the rescue dog that survived against all the odds. So long as our Leo isn't upstaged, its heart will embrace its chosen companion totally and see it as an extension of its wonderful self.

Features

Love: Leos are capable of great passion and intense adoration if the relationship is going well. If it's not... well... who likes being caged up with a sullen or even angry lion! However, when people or dogs are right for them, they will give their hearts completely and forever.

Money: Willing to work flat out to get the recognition and status they need means that success can often follow. Ambition drives them on when lesser mortals would drop by the wayside. Being a good boss, they need a colleague who can cope with the mundane tasks that drive Leos to distraction.

Health: Needing to take care of their hearts (all that excitement!), walking the dog and having a cuddle can be very therapeutic for our Leos. A close canine companion can also be an early warning system for those untoward accidents to which Leos can be prone.

K9 Tips

Don't give your dog grapes or raisins; they can't metabolise some of the content, and it can lead to kidney damage!

Not mentioned in many pet books - check with your Vet.

Sun Sign Virgo

Dates: August 23 to September 22
Planet: Mercury
Symbol: The Maiden
Gender: Feminine
Element: Earth
Quality: Mutable
Colour: Lavender
Gem: Amethyst

The Virgo Dog

August 23 to September 22

We are talking about cleanliness here. More than any other dog in the universe, your delightful Virgo dog requires clean, tidy surroundings and that includes you, dear owner! This dog needs well-prepared and nutritious food served at regular intervals and walks that you can set your watch by. With delicate digestive systems, they need set routines to ensure they are able to go to the loo regularly, or they may get bunged up, which will land you with endless vet visits and an anxious pet… a very anxious pet!

These are clever, quick-witted dogs and they are very loyal, so they will never desert you for a more interesting option. Indeed, you may find Virgo dogs watching you out of the corner of their eye and nothing will slide past them. You may think you can slip out the door quietly, only to find them shadowing you, an inch behind you.

Equally, they know when you are down, and they will be there for you in their quiet, unassuming and loving way.They appreciate it when you talk to them, and they can learn a great number of words.

Use this talent and talk, talk, talk!

The Virgo Dog

The Virgo Owner

August 23 to September 22

What can I say about the most wonderful sign of the zodiac? You can guess what sign I am, and my darling husband and my dog? Yes, productive, efficient, reliable and loving Virgo - what's not to love? Mmm…

Okay, so Virgos can be a bit picky, perfectionist and just a tad controlling, but we are a loving, humorous sign that is great at training both the humans and dogs in our lives. Of course, they might not want to be trained, but that's another story!

A Virgo's dog will be well-fed, well-exercised and well-trained (I know, I've done it quite a few times). The more a Virgo person is loved, the higher their self-esteem grows, so a loving dog is a great benefit. Snappy, aloof dogs need not apply. Chaos can unnerve a Virgo, so having a dog that is willing to be trained is vital.

Features

Love: Virgos can be alluring folk in a loving, supportive relationship. This is where they can operate confidently and be at their scintillating best. Difficult relationships with humans or dogs bring out their super-controlling and deeply anxious side and need to be avoided.

Money: Having an analytical mind and a capacity to multi-task, these people can create stable, successful enterprises and make great employees. These qualities keep them off the breadline and ensure their doggie companions have proper care, food and vet checkups.

Health: Constantly living up to high standards and always aiming to get things right can leave Virgos stressed out. Nervous digestive complaints can ensue. Healing happens when there is time to chill out. A silly game in the park with a dog can be very healing indeed!

K9 Tips
Use a good harness with your leash;
leash clipped to a collar can hurt your pet.

Sun Sign Libra

Dates:	September 23 to October 22
Planet:	Venus
Symbol:	The Scales
Gender:	Masculine
Element:	Air
Quality:	Cardinal
Colours:	Pink or green
Gem:	Rose quartz

The Libra Dog

Act rationally and calmly around this animal and they become easy to have around. Even-tempered and amiable, they like you - their love object - to be the same. A pleasant home and a serene atmosphere suit them the most. Serenity appeals to them and they can be bothered by loud, unexpected noises and a disturbed environment.

They will pick up any worries you have and act on them – worrying at things and situations and having a good old whine and whimper, showing a sorry lack of confidence and generally wanting to hide under the bed!

Unlike other dogs, this one can have the greatest difficulty making up its mind, and under extreme stress, may start going in circles and biting its tail! It is your job to give clear and strong guidance in a gentle and loving tone. Make sure it is trained to return to you when you go out and take the dog off the lead, and make your instructions clear.

You will need to build this dog's confidence, make sure it is surrounded by calmness and ensure that it can rely on you to provide the security and stability it so badly needs! Once this is done, you will dearly love this animal and its devotion to you.

Reassure, reassure, reassure!

The Libra Dog

The Libra Owner

September 23 to October 22
Diplomacy meets fairness, and gracefulness meets amiability in this easy-going sign. So amiable that others can take advantage. Librans have a capacity to take criticism to heart and they can put themselves down into the bargain.

This sign needs creative expression as much as they need harmony and a sense of equilibrium. Noisy, barking, disruptive dogs will need to mend their ways if they want to wheedle their way into a Libran's heart.

Loyal and generous, Librans have a lot of love to give. The most reasonable of all the signs, they have their breaking point. A gentle, well-mannered and sociable dog would suit a Libran. A companion that behaves itself and fits peacefully into a peaceful household would benefit this sign.

Features

Love: Librans can fall in love easily and respond well to displays of affection. Memo to prospective dog... wag your tail a lot on meeting a potential owner! Harmonious relationships are very important to this sign. Coarse behaviour from a human or dog will win no hearts, quite the reverse!

Money: Being both intelligent and fair as well as creative, many careers open up to Librans, and although they are not driven by the acquisition of money, they can carve careers out of many differing avenues, such as the arts and the law.

Health: Unfair treatment and a deep tendency to worry can stress out our Libran friends. Imbalances, disharmony and conflicts add to the stress toll. De-stressing, keeping balanced and centred help this sign regain its calm centre. Librans need a good quality diet.

K9 Tips
Winter coming up?
Your dog will appreciate
a warm, waterproof coat.

Sun Sign Scorpio

Dates: October 23 to November 21
Planet: Pluto
Symbol: The Scorpion
Gender: Feminine
Element: Water
Quality: Fixed
Colour: Dark red
Gem: Black onyx

The Scorpio Dog

October 23 to November 21
Coo… you're in for a ride here. Not given to half measures, this is a mesmerising animal that gets lots of notice on the streets. This dog is impossible to ignore.

Expert at reading body language (yours!), it demands attention, love and complete adoration. You will find that your pet can be jealous, and it is not averse to giving the odd nip here and there to warn off competition. From the word go, you have to be firm, or the role of pack leader will go to Scorpio dog and stay there.

This is a clever dog; you won't find it boring, and you will enjoy engaging its astute mind. Make no mistake, Scorpio dog will love you deeply and profoundly. This makes up for when it feels thwarted and when it can plummet into a depressed state.

Should this happen, you must find ways to manage its needs, and do this kindly and very firmly. This dog needs to feel completely at one with you, so a good strategy is to give it as much one-to-one time as you can. Attention to your Scorpio pet will never go amiss. At least once a day, make it feel like it is the only thing in your life.

Attention, attention, attention!

The Scorpio Dog

The Scorpio Owner

October 23 to November 21
Scorpios can get bad press. They are passionate, volatile and single-minded – a good person to have in one's corner when things get tough. But those very traits, if taken to extremes, can result in difficult situations and relationships; not always, it must be said. Loyal to the last, if a Scorpio commits to a rescue dog that has issues, that dog will never be abandoned, come what may.

They can make great champions and once locked onto a cause will see it through. Of course, inflexibility can work against them on occasion, but if a Scorpio falls in love with a dog, it's for life!

This is a sensual sign that responds well to the physical affection of a large dog, and if it's dramatic looking, well and good. The relationship between dog and human will be intense and the more intense the dog appears to be, so much the better.

Features

Love: Scorpios long for deep, profound and earth-shattering relationships. Theatrical and dramatic, these people are often not exactly easy. Fulfilling and wonderful with the right person, they can be the stuff of newspaper headlines if they go wrong.

Money: Industrious if their fascination is engaged and if the work matters to them, this sign can be eminently successful. The world of dark and mysterious matters draws them, so consequently the range of occupations is wide-ranging, from the life-affirming to the downright criminal!

Health: With such a serious, intense and intuitive sign, emotional difficulties can bring on digestive disorders and headaches, to name but a few. A deep connection with their doggie companion can bring comfort and love to them when things look dark.

K9 Tips
Pet insurance is worth it!
check the cost of common accident
treatments - you'll be surprised!

Sun Sign Sagittarius

Dates: November 22 to December 21
Planet: Jupiter
Symbol: The Centaur
Gender: Masculine
Element: Fire
Quality: Mutable
Colour: Purple
Gem: Sodalite

The Sagittarius Dog

November 22 to December 21
There is something odd about Sagittarian dogs because however much you groom them and however many chic little doggie outfits you buy them, they always manage to look... well... odd! Hair that sticks up, weird, sideways movements, and a wild rolling of the eyes characterise the strange Sagittarian dog.

This is a cheerful animal, and curiosity courses through its veins, leading it into challenging situations without a second thought. Free-spirited and lively, these dogs seem to land on their feet unscathed, after all manner of near misses, but they need watching for that one time in a million when things can go awry.

Despite their seemingly boundless enthusiasm, they need time to bond with you, so let them get to know you. Also, their energy is not endless; they sometimes need to collapse and recuperate. These dogs have an independent streak and are quite happy to root around in strange places on their own, but you must check that the places aren't too strange; this dog knows no fear, and you may have to do a fair bit of rescuing.

Watch, watch, watch.

The Sagittarius Dog

The Sagittarius Owner

November 22 to December 21

Welcome to free-spirited and independent Sagittarius. Here we have an adventurer never happier than when on a quest, be it physical, emotional or mental – and often a combination of them all!

This level of restless activity can sometimes result in carelessness and chaos. This is not the best sign for a dog that needs pampering, that wants to be the centre of attention or is unable to go with the flow. Sagittarian folk are intelligent, optimistic people who value their independence, and yet they can be used by less scrupulous family members.

A happy dog, which is an equally free-spirited dog, will be forgiven all manner of misdemeanours if it can match its owner's high energy and doesn't mind meals being at erratic times. The Sagittarian needs a self-sufficient dog, able to forgive the lack of grooming, walks at strange times and the inevitable unplanned and unusual trips.

Features

Love: Given their propensity for freedom, lovers need to be understanding friends as well as partners. They will attract potential Sagittarian partners by being witty, outgoing and exciting. Whether the companion is a dog or a human, joining in with the Sagittarian's expansive lifestyle will work, rather than trying to curtail it.

Money: Material success does not loom large in importance here. It may well happen, but it won't be the goal. This is a sign that loves to learn and be involved with work that really matters in the world. Someone at hand who can handle the details is a definite asset.

Health: Sagittarians are so busy on their quests that seemingly minor issues can end up being ignored. Meals grabbed on the run can result in fuller waistlines, and poor diets can take their toll health-wise. Be sure to attend to health checks.

K9 Tips
A little address tag on your dog's collar is invaluable; dogs are easily lost.

Sun Sign Capricorn

Dates: December 22 to January 20
Planet: Saturn
Symbol: The Goat
Gender: Feminine
Element: Earth
Quality: Cardinal
Colour: Brown
Gem: Tiger's eye

The Capricorn Dog

December 22 to January 20

Not immediately demonstrative, this dog is deceptive and - like still waters that run deep - there is much depth to this dog's nature. Emotional dogs when you get to know them (that may take time and energy,), so be patient and consistent with them.

Train your Capricorn dog well and encourage it to be useful, because it will enjoy being so. They benefit from a bit of loosening up, so cuddles and tummy rubs are in order.

If yours is a rescue dog, they may have had a challenging time in the past, and they may be a bit more serious than your average youngster, so tender, loving care will help cement your bond.

This dog can be a bit reserved and even timid, so plenty of exercise with an emphasis on fun works wonders. They need to be encouraged to play.

You will have had to work to get close to them (it's well worth it!), but strangers may find themselves out in the cold, especially if they indulge in baby, doggie talk, as all they'll get is a sarcastic eye lift and a hard stare.

This dog's affection is not easily bought, and being rather conservative, it can turn its face to the wall when things get too over the top. Think "Maiden Aunt" with a sensuous side!

Respect, respect, respect!

The Capricorn Dog

Capricorn Owner

December 22 to January 20

Welcome to someone who knows the rules, keeps to the rules and indeed often writes them. Yes, its Capricorn. Still waters run deep here. Despite a sometimes-forbidding exterior, they feel things intensely, although they may suffer in silence… for a while!

Practical and determined, their canine pal will be trained to within an inch of its life, whether it wants to be or not! They will be fed, walked and their overall care will be exemplary. Not a fan of bad behaviour; barkers, chewers and random accident makers must beware! Naughtiness will not be looked on kindly, and back they will go to training sessions!

Fortunately, Capricorns have a ready wit, and once bonded with a like-minded human or animal, can prove to be devoted. Not averse to a good cuddle, this is a good owner, though a demanding one.

Features

Love: Not interested in dramas of any sort, Capricorns can be both loving and faithful when they connect with a confident, and in their eyes, worthy partner. They take life seriously, though a partner who can lighten the atmosphere won't go amiss.

Money: Given their ability to focus and plan, Capricorns are unlikely to be poor. They take the acquisition of money very seriously, and prosperity appeals to them. They can be workaholics and they have high expectations of themselves and of those around them.

Health: All that seriousness and too much work can sometimes result in depression and anxiety, so loosening up a bit works wonders. A happy welcome from a canine companion, a walk to let go of the day's stresses and a bit of toy throwing can work wonders!

K9 Tips

Grapes and raisins aren't the only thing you should avoid giving your loyal and trusting pet:
Look online for much more information about how best to care for your K9 companion.

Sun Sign Aquarius

Dates: January 21 to February 18
Planet: Uranus
Symbol: The Water Carrier
Gender: Masculine
Element: Air
Quality: Fixed
Colour: Bright blue
Gem: Lapis lazuli

The Aquarius Dog

January 21 to February 18

A strange being... this dog looks like it's from another planet and it doesn't quite understand the rules of earth! Independent and unconventional, ordinary training is a hit-and-miss affair, so adopting an unconventional approach may work wonders.

As this is a dog with a lively, inventive mind, you can allow yourself to adopt an offbeat approach; teach them unusual skills that require concentration, and when they get the idea, praise them loudly and repeatedly. This is a friendly and happy dog that enjoys being around a lot of people, as long as they are not too needy or boring.

These dogs may appear a bit too independent at times, but do not take this as rejection, because it isn't – a natural detachment is part of this dog's makeup.

This is a far from shallow dog; explore its intelligence, then you will find a very smart dog that will join you in all manner of unusual activities. So, if you want to walk up a mountain or play in the adventure playground in the park, your Aquarian dog will happily join in.

Engage, engage, engage!

The Aquarius Dog

The Aquarius Owner

January 21 to February 18
Welcome to the agile-minded, humanitarian and high-principled Aquarian. Although your mental processes may be hard to follow, for those who plod in your wake, you are capable of the most amazing insights.

You are not afraid of the future and of technology, but rather inspired and drawn to these challenges. Because Aquarians believe in equality and will work for the rights of all, animal welfare can figure highly on their agenda. The cause of alleviating the suffering of dogs being puppy farmed, used for breeding, hunting or racing may take precedence over an individual dog.

Having said that, rescuing a dog from a far-off war-torn country or a three-legged unwanted dog left in a rescue centre could directly appeal to Aquarian sensibilities. As could using their animal to highlight the plight of others and to work for change.

Features

Love: If love is mixed with friendship, then intimate relationships have a better chance of success. Fiercely independent and averse to neediness, Aquarians can be seen as aloof. Potential lovers need both patience and understanding to plumb the Aquarian depths.

Money: As pushing the limits of technology is enjoyable and ideas for the future are enthralling, Aquarians may well enjoy success in beating their own path towards tomorrow. Cultivating flexibility can balance out getting stuck in fixed ideas. They love to guide and teach others.

Health: An eccentric, energetic lifestyle leaves little time for self-care, so attention to diet and exercise is vital both for physical and mental health. Blood circulation can be troublesome, and leg ulcers are possible later in life. This sign can harbour self-doubts and in consequence, suffer mood swings.

K9 Tips
Before buying or taking on a new dog, check if it is safe with children and other dogs & cats.

Sun Sign Pisces

Dates: February 19 to March 20
Planet: Neptune
Symbol: The Fishes
Gender: Feminine
Element: Water
Quality: Mutable
Colour: Sea blue/green
Gem: Turquoise

The Pisces Dog

February 19 to March 20
This is a sensitive little critter! Your Pisces dog will quiver with attention at all your nuances and be totally tuned in to you. It is deeply sympathetic to your needs. Also, your Pisces dog can be adversely affected by rows and upsets, so keep a watchful eye out for that.

Not the absolutely sharpest tool in the toolbox, it sometimes gets things wrong. This is a dog with so much imagination, it can get lost in a sea of wonderings, so when out and about, it might be best to use one of those long leads, as it can literally get lost!

A little bit gullible, this dog can be led astray by unscrupulous people and by other animals, and it can find itself in difficult situations from which it will need rescuing! (This is your job). On the upside, this is a faithful and very loving dog that will adore you for the whole of its life and it will feel like a part of you.

It needs your guidance, and it will continue this need for the whole of your time together. You will grow very close to this gentle dog, and it will love you unreservedly and forever – just keep your eyes out for it!

Guard, guard, guard!

The Pisces Dog

The Pisces Owner

February 19 to March 20
The most imaginative, sensitive and vulnerable sign of the
zodiac… say welcome to Pisces. Empathetic to a vast
degree, boundaries need to be established super quickly!

Generous and loving, our Pisceans friends can be sucked
into unwanted situations that they simply do not seem to
fully perceive. Sometimes tripped up by their urge to take
care of others and to be taken care of, they can stumble into
being exploited.

The love of a good dog can heal and give much-needed
support, though dogs need to be trained or they will assume
the role of pack leader. I've seen this happen!

However, when their wonderful imaginations are harnessed to
something Pisceans can totally believe in, this can lead to real
and lasting fulfilment for themselves and those they love.

Features

Love: These are loving people who constantly see the best (even when it's not there!) in those they adore. Developing the skill to face reality, or creating a supportive group to help them see the truth, will help them to deal with the practicalities of life.

Work: Pisceans need to develop the skills needed to use their incredible creativity and imagination. They can create big visionary concepts (that imagination!) and with the right skills and support can be incredibly successful in the arts, but also in a sales capacity.

Health: Illnesses can be emotionally based in such a sensitive sign. With a delicate constitution, finding ways to handle worry and combat it as much as possible is a must. A faithful and loving dog can bring the unreserved affection so needed by a Piscean.

Zodiac Dogs

K9 Tips
Some innocent-looking doggies are
masters at escaping from your back
or front garden.
Not fair to mention specific breeds,
so I won't mention Beagles...
Make sure your property's fence /
wall perimeter is sound.

Doggie Historical Background

40,000 to 20,000 BCE: Some wolves begin to change and become dog-like.

15,000 BCE: Dogs become a separate species from ancient wolves.

14, 223 BCE: Evidence of humans owning dogs.

12,000 to 10,000 BCE: Dogs get smaller and more like modern dogs. Definite evidence of dogs living with humans.

9,500 BCE: Arctic dogs being used to pull sledges over long distances.

7,000 BCE: Some ancient dog poo rediscovered in modern times.

3,300 to 600 BCE: Cave paintings of dogs.

1873: The Kennel Club is formed in the UK to standardise breeds.

1938: Eric Knight writes a short story about a rough collie called Lassie. This turns up in a full-length novel in 1940 and Lassie becomes the heroine of films and TV programmes in the USA and also the UK.

Zodiac Dogs

1944: The then Princess Elizabeth's father, King George VI gives her a corgi that she calls Susie. Susie is protective of her owner but notoriously unfriendly to the palace staff. Many more generations of corgis follow after Susie.

2022: The last two of the late Queen Elizabeth's corgis are being cared for by other members of the Royal Family.

Princess Anne is known for her love of the English Bull Terrier, and King Charles has two rescue Jack Russell Terriers.

The Elements

So here we have the dogs that range from lively Aries to sensitive Pisces. What happens when they collide with humans, when they bring their personalities and energies into our homes and lives? Do we instantly fall in love with each other or do we eye each other up over the chewed slippers, little accidents on the best rug and the abject refusal to walk on the lead? The truth is often somewhere in the middle, and remember love will conquer all... along with lots of training!

As a Virgo owner (four planets in Virgo, I might add!), I probably need to accept that good behaviour is a must, and my responsibility is to train my pooches and not expect them to understand why their food dish needs to be in that particular place on that particular mat AT ALL TIMES! My poodle Snowy was as picky as my Virgoan husband and I were, and if that food bowl was moved from its usual spot, we got the hard stare until it was back in its rightful place! I always felt that Snowy was a fellow Virgo.

I knew an Aries owner with an Aries dog, and in this case it was a marriage made in heaven, but no one else got a look in. It was a messy and joyfully, happy affair. Very, very messy though, and chaotic. Did I mention chaotic! But they were off having adventures, living on a boat, going to parties, wearing identical neckerchiefs and having a ball. I drew the dog for its owner and when it sadly died, she mourned it more than any person she had ever lost.

I have a very dear Libran friend. She is diplomatic to her core and easy-going. Did I mention she's a hard worker who works from home? Did I also mention she is averse to pets of any kind? She grew up on a farm and to her, animals are animals and they belong outside, but also sometimes served up with a tasty sauce. So along came a small, elderly dog that had been temporarily abandoned. She rang me, perplexed and wondering what to do with it. Apparently, she and the dog had stared at each other for a while, and while taking in her calming Libran atmosphere, it kept coming closer, to sit, leaning against her.

She needed this dog to be calm, to fit in with her routine and not get in the way of her work, while the dog needed comfort and stability. She decided the dog might benefit from having its own bed, somewhere comfy and warm, and she positioned it on her feet while she worked. Peace was established; they both got what they wanted and her final comment on the situation was, "Actually, he's a very sweet little fellow".

It's important to meet both human and dog needs.

I mention this story because we potential dog owners need to get very clear what we need and want from a dog. Very, very clear!!!

So how does this marriage of humans and dogs work?

Do remember as we go on this journey, where humans meet dogs, there are many factors in a horoscope, as indeed in life, that make us what we are; the sun sign is only one of these. So how to understand this magical universe in which we all live us humans and animals?

The Astrological Elements

Well, first of all, lets do a bit of ground work by meeting the elements.

The signs of the zodiac are grouped into four different elements. They are Fire, Earth, Air and Water. Each element group contains three of the sun signs, and although each sign has different characteristics, they all share the same basic energy of the element in which they reside.

Fire

Aries, Leo and Sagittarius

Boom! First we meet the element of Fire, which brings that first vital explosion of energy. Both animals and humans born in this element have the capacity to bring courage, excitement and desire, to say nothing of enthusiasm. There's an excitement here – a burning brightly, though as with everything under the sun, there can be a shadow side. Namely, in this case, a certain restlessness and a tendency to kick over boundaries along with a troublesome tendency to literally burn out and end up as a pile of ashes. Let's take a quick peep at the Fire signs and what they might want and need.

Aries

Hello Aries...well you might want a dog to share your love of adventure, to be up for anything and to be ready to join you in the race to be first. You can have competitive tendencies and you need to guard against entering into a confrontation with your pooch. Remember, even if you are both scaling a mountain or power walking, your dog will need love and attention, and there will be times when one or the other of you feels insecure (yes, it does happen to Aries!). Allow your doggie soul mate to comfort you and be ready to give them a reassuring cuddle when its needed. I know you need to feel you are the boss, but you must remember your dog may occasionally need to feel like the pack leader!

Leo

I know you Leos demand loyalty and you give it in spades, too. Remember when dealing with your furry friend that they may chew your new, brightly coloured rug or forget their toilet training in a frenzy of excitement, but it doesn't mean they're disloyal to you... they just need more training. Also, given your lively, energetic and charismatic nature, you may forget that your pet needs time to chill and relax, and that won't hurt you, either. You have a furry companion to train and dress up, which will show you both to your best advantage. Together, you can both cut glamorous figures, so you have a potential team here. Allow your animal companion to take centre stage occasionally, and remember that their glory is your glory! Take time to bask in their adoration, as it's there for you, and you know how much you love to be adored!

Sagittarius

You like your pals, and you will have a pal in your dog, so if you take on a puppy, your natural optimism will carry you over the bumpy youngster period. You will bounce back from training setbacks, though you will need to set realistic goals for both you and your dog and stick to them. You are the pack leader, so don't get swayed from training routines and avoid procrastinating over establishing boundaries. You will always need your own space at times, so a dog that enjoys their own company on occasion will work well for you. If your dog is too needy, you may need to train it out of separation anxiety. You will thoroughly enjoy the laughter that a dog brings into your life and the stories of your dog escapades that you can share and enjoy with others.

Earth

Taurus, Virgo and Capricorn
Where Fire gets "earthed" it becomes something real and tangible. The energy enters its stable, productive and dependable states. On the up side for both animals and humans, these signs are deeply sensual, physical and they can get things done. Of course, there is our old friend, the shadow side, who pops up as a tendency to get bogged down in practical matters, and stuck in a rut that is so deep it can resemble a grave.

Taurus

You bring stamina and persistence to your role as a dog owner. Dependable and protective of your pooch you're also pleasure-loving, and all those cuddles are not wasted on you or your dog. Grounded in reality, you will be aware of the commitment you're taking on and the energy and foresight it requires. Your dogged (!) determination will see you through the training and help you establish solid routines for you and your canine companion. A lively dog will help keep you lively in turn, and stop any tendency to fall into a rut and become too set in your ways. You are a creature of pleasure, and the joys of the table can sometimes beckon a tad too strongly, so avoid piling on those extra pounds – I'm talking about both you AND your dog! Having said that, you know you enjoy the familiar and the domestic. Having a dog be part of that will enhance it, and the security of the love a

The Astrological Elements

dog can bring into your life is the icing on the cake – just avoid eating too much of it!

Virgo

Hello, quick-witted Virgo! Can you tell I'm a Virgo? Well we are particular, sensitive and totally wonderful… only kidding! I know Virgos can be classed as critical and nitpicking, but we are also kind, generous and loyal. With a dog, we will be aware of the need to train. In my case, I borrowed a few books out of the library before my dog arrived. Once we know what to do, we apply ourselves to the tasks in hand with commitment and kindness. An adventurous dog or a super lively one will keep us on our toes, as will all those walks, which are good for relieving the stresses Virgos can sometimes endure. Virgos are good at managing their dogs' health and good at researching any ailments their animals might have. Just one note of caution, fellow Virgos; avoid nagging… the poor pooch is doing its best!

Capricorn

You are responsible… very responsible, so you know the rules and follow them. You might appear more serious than other people, but deep down happiness is there and a dog can help you access your joy. You know what needs to be done as a dog owner, and you do everything to ensure all is well, from investing in good insurance to buying sturdy leads and nutritious food. Your dog will appreciate your patience, and as a natural leader, you will have no difficulty assuming the mantle of pack leader. With your air of authority, training your dog will come naturally to you, and your dog should respond accordingly. Let yourself go occasionally, be a bit silly and allow your earthy sensuality to combat any tendencies towards feeling low. Remember - getting a doggie hug can lift your spirits as well as relaxing and comforting you when you need it.

Air

Gemini, Libra and Aquarius
Here comes Air, adding reasoning and understanding to the mix, and being on an intellectual search for life's meaning. Driven by curiosity and the need to grapple with big ideas and solve the big conundrums, here are the networkers of the universe. There is a shadow side of course, this time lurking with its head up in the clouds so that it is detached from life and stuck in its objectivity.

Gemini

With your quick inquisitive mind and your clever nature, training your dog can be the challenge you've been yearning for, and in your up-to-date training methods, you could have a doggie winner on your hands. Being gregarious, you'll enjoy the company and laughter shared with other dog owners. However, keep up that good quality training and avoid getting bored by focusing your attention on your doggie companion, and celebrating its achievements with all and sundry. Maybe vary the training too, from time to time. Liking to be active and on the move, you ought occasionally to stop and smell the roses and give that dog a cuddle. You never stop learning and neither will your dog if you make a point of continuing to elevate its intelligence as well as your own.

Libra

Librans are such a restful sign to me. With your even temper and diplomatic nature, you would welcome an animal into your life with love, and provide it with a restful environment. However, its not all roses though, as a noisy dog could throw you into a conniption and a messy one would make you severely upset. Dogs don't always start out as the harmonious creatures they may later become, so choosing your companion wisely and giving good training are paramount. Take time to consider what size and personality you would need. A dog by your side can help ease the worries that sometimes beset you, and their undying love can boost the times that your self esteem takes a dive. Harmony in your life is vital, so when making room for a dog, consider how to establish the tranquillity you crave, and pick your best pal accordingly.

Aquarius

You will bring your altruistic and future-orientated mind into dog ownership. You will always see the bigger picture and care deeply about nature and the planet, so your dog will have the most natural and nutritious food you can buy, and its bed will be made of the most ethical material. In your urge to help our beautiful planet survive and not waste resources, you may well go for a rescue dog. Its true you can be eccentric and lead an unusual life, but dogs accept us for what we are; if given love and care, they will follow us to the ends of the earth and consider themselves privileged. A dog relationship may well dispel any hidden self doubt you may have lurking, and when you bond with your dog, it will be forever – and that will work both ways.

Water

Cancer, Scorpio and Pisces
Water flows in, bringing sensitivity and acute empathy. The universe needs such intuitive and often psychic beings, as they bring their own brand of gentle compassion to the world. Water sign animals and humans are very responsive and in tune with everything around them. And yet, here's that shadow that brings with it a swamp of emotions so sticky it's hard to climb out of, and in worst case scenarios, a total lack of objectivity.

Cancer

Being an emotionally sensitive sign you have a strong sense of your inner life and strangely enough, of your outer one too. Very intuitive and able to make strong ties of love, a dog will be cherished and adored by you. Your doggie pal will be welcomed into a caring home, and that will mean all the world to you. You will stick by your dog through thick and thin and never give up on it, no matter what. I know a Cancerian who has spent a fortune on dog trainers, while helping a very distressed dog through early traumas so that it could start to live its best life, and she will never hear a bad word said about the pooch. This is a lovely thing, but you must remember that you are the pack leader, and as such, you need to take control and establish rules as well as giving support and assistance. Your ability to love is amazing but you must remember not to cling too possessively.

Scorpio

Wow - what a passionate, entrancing sign you are! You like to live life to the full and you would want your dog to be as full of life as you are, and to be as engaged with life. Together you will make an eye catching pair, both of you striding along the road, being the centre of attention, and commanding the room wherever you both go. Choose your animal companion wisely so as to be in tune with what you want and need. Also give both yourself and your dog time out from the intensity of your relationship and the full-on life that you lead, and allow both of you to have interludes of solitude that will replenish you and draw you both closer together. The faithfulness and adoration of your dog will then fulfil a deep need inside of you.

Pisces

So sensitive and emotionally aware that your capacity to bond with your dog is legendary. At times you can feel as though you are one being. Generous with your time, energy and such money as you have, you will need to learn to establish boundaries or the role of pack leader will not be yours, because a little furry head will be wearing that crown!

A Piscean woman I know was so in thrall to her very small dog that she would pick it up whenever it yapped. In the end, it chose not even to walk across the room to its food bowl, so in effect, she became its servant. For both of you to be happy and healthy, you need to take responsibility for both of you and to stick to the rules that need to be followed. You will always see the best in your dog and you can inspire profound love. A lifetime companion will boost your self esteem and if things get tough, your doggie will get you out of bed in the morning.

Calling All
Zodiac Dog Owners!

Yes, that means you too, Aries. Stop and concentrate, Gemini for just one minute. Don't look so serious, Capricorn. There are some things we all owe our dogs.

Firstly: Do think seriously about what you want from your doggie companion... be honest now, Scorpio! It may be more than one thing. Just because your dog is a star on Instagram doesn't mean you don't want love and comfort from it as well. The dog might figure in your work as a conservationist Aquarius, but it can also bring you the deep companionship and peace you crave. Be clear with yourself and your dog.

So, if you tick more than one topic below, that's fine.

Do you want:

- Unconditional love
- Play and fun
- Adventure and excitement
- Calmness
- Protection
- Intelligence

Calling All Zodiac Dog Owners!

- Companionship
- Obedience
- Good looks
- An Instagram star

Secondly: train your dog, whether you are about to buy a new dog or if you already have one. Now, people of some signs of the zodiac will take to this easily (hello Virgo) while others may struggle (yes, I'm talking to you, Pisces). However, we all need to remember our canine buddies are not little people in furry suits, but animals that do much better in our world when they are trained.

Thirdly: research the breed and the background of the dog you want, so you know what you are getting into. This information, teamed with the zodiac signs, can give you a real insight into the hound in your life. An excitable Gemini cockapoo could be very different to an excitable Taurean cockapoo. The former might well be bouncing off the walls whilst the latter might just wag their tail a lot!

The relationship with your dog is a long-lasting one that brings so much joy. We owe it to our dogs as well as to ourselves to do our research and to give them our leadership in the form of training, in addition to giving them our love and care.

K9 Tips
Do train your dog, or hire a trainer;
It's never too late to train.
Your neighbours might not tell you,
but a dog that barks day & night is
incredibly stressful for other
people.
Be considerate to others ...

Dogs on the Cusp

If a dog is born on the cusp between two signs - and particularly if it is born towards the end of a sign - it can display characteristics of both signs. Much the same goes for people, as those born towards the end of a sign start to pick up characteristics from the next sign along.

LIST OF CUSPS	
ARIES	TAURUS
TAURUS	GEMINI
GEMINI	CANCER
CANCER	LEO
LEO	VIRGO
VIRGO	LIBRA
LIBRA	SCORPIO
SCORPIO	SAGITTARIUS
SAGITTARIUS	CAPRICORN
CAPRICORN	AQUARIUS
AQUARIUS	PISCES
PISCES	ARIES

K9 Tips

Use a special doggie seatbelt clip in the car; they are cheap and will minimise harm if braking hard. Also, it won't let you pet jump out the window.

Compatibility Chart for
People and Dogs

The fun chart overleaf shows the compatibility between signs, which might apply to people and their dogs, or to two people or to two dogs.

Three stars – Brilliant!
Two stars   – Good.
One star   – Poor.

Zodiac Dogs

	Aries	Taurus	Gemini	Cancer	Leo	Virgo	Libra	Scorpio	Sagittarius	Capricorn	Aquarius	Pisces
Aries	3	2	3	1	3	1	1	2	3	1	2	1
Taurus	2	3	2	3	1	3	2	2	1	3	1	2
Gemini	3	2	3	2	2	2	3	1	3	1	3	2
Cancer	1	3	2	3	1	3	2	3	1	2	1	3
Leo	3	1	2	1	3	2	3	1	3	1	2	1
Virgo	1	3	2	2	2	3	2	2	1	3	2	3
Libra	1	2	3	2	3	2	3	2	2	2	2	2
Scorpio	2	2	1	3	1	2	2	3	2	3	2	3
Sagittarius	3	1	3	1	3	1	2	2	3	1	3	2
Capricorn	1	3	2	2	1	3	2	3	1	3	2	3
Aquarius	2	1	3	1	2	2	2	2	3	2	3	1
Pisces	1	2	2	3	1	3	2	3	2	3	1	3

Conclusion

This book is a tribute to the interconnected, magical universe we live in, and whatever species we are, we all deserve respect and care.

That's the serious bit over with, so I hope this book brings a smile, maybe the occasional chuckle and a wee bit of information to you and that you enjoy taking a closer look at our furry friends and how we relate to them. Love is a truly incredible gift, and dogs give that to us without reservation.

K9 Tips

Your dog's claws may need clipping from time to time.
If you're not experienced, have it done by the Vet; clipping too far back may cut into the "quick", hurting your pet and exposing it to infection.

Top Reviews
for Zodiac Dogs!

"This is a really good tail!"
Bruno the Boxer

"I'm cutting my teeth, so this book will make a great doggie chew..."
Larry the young Lurcher

"Now that Jane has finished slaving over her magnum opus, maybe she'll find time to take me for a nice long walk."
Rocky the rescue mutt

"This is a truly rotten book!!
Connie the Cat

Milton Keynes UK
Ingram Content Group UK Ltd.
UKHW051155080923
428286UK00003B/5

9 781903 065976